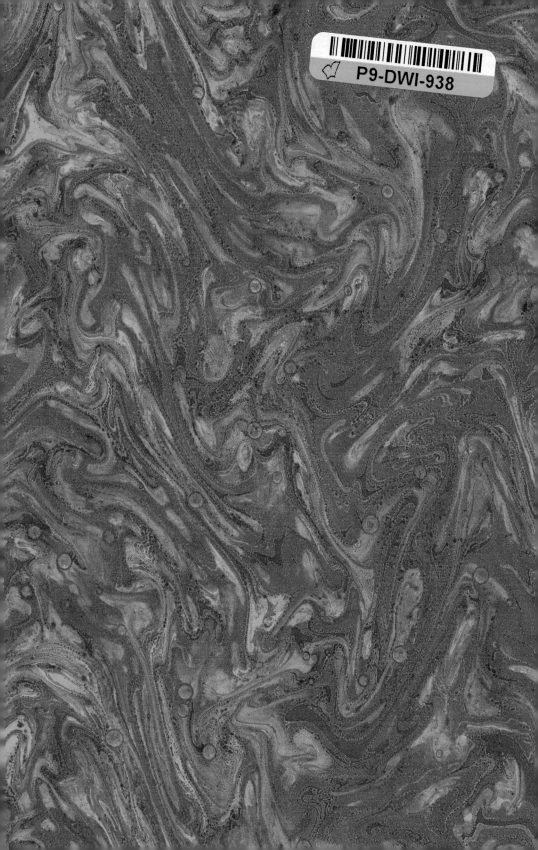

TRINERGY

TRINER

TABULA RASA PRESS   MORRO B.

GY

A SELECTION OF
POEMS BY
GORDON CURZON

ILLUSTRATIONS BY
LES GRAY

A COLLECTION OF
POEMS IN THREE BOOKS:

AMERICAN ANTHOLOGY
CHICAGO MEMORIES
CALIFORNIA and BEYOND

CALIFORNIA

1986

ISBN 0-931943-03-5

For C J

"Poetry is what in a poem makes you laugh, cry,
twist your toes, twinkle, prickle, be silent,
know you are alone and not alone
in an unknown world."

— Dylan Thomas

ACKNOWLEDGEMENTS

Some of the poems in this collection have appeared
in the following:

A Quarterly Journal of California Poetry and Art
The California State Poetry Quarterly
The Bellingham Review
The Illinois Quarterly
Franciscan Message
Studia Mystica
Laudamus Te
The Archer
Cafe Solo
Manifold
Motive
Impact

ABOUT THE AUTHOR

GORDON CURZON was born into an old English family, March 14, 1919. His birth home still stands in Surrey, not far south of London. He came to America as an immigrant, among the last to go through Ellis Island. He lost his English accent in public school in Cleveland, Ohio. It was in Chicago, Illinois he grew up. He received his first degree (in chemistry) from De Paul University just before Pearl Harbor. After a long stint as a research chemist he switched careers at 48 and earned a doctorate in English from the University of California. He is the co-founder of the California State Poetry Society and the founding editor of the California State Poetry Quarterly now in its fifteenth year. He has had over a hundred publications here and abroad. He is now professor of English at California Polytechnic State University in San Luis Obispo. He and his wife, a published musician, composer and teacher live in Shell Beach. Their four children are all pursuing their own careers in science, music, writing and the law.

FOREWORD

THOSE OF US WHO by choice come to fruition later in life will never share the experience of poets who flower early, expire, leaving behind their poems as epitaph.

In compensation, the later life poet with less immediate satisfaction in the halcyon early years has the incomparable satisfaction of artistic fulfillment when he can appreciate, enjoy and savour it most.

Gordon Curzon, I venture to suggest, belongs to this breed of poets with a late publication of poems matured like good wine over the years, and, finally realised; and, in his self-descriptive terms, he, as "an aspiring, elderly poet" has now the opportunity to share his poems with other poetry buffs.

Drawn from so many different threads of life, his poems are consistently approachable. I like in particular "Epitaph" and "California Christmas," both down to earth, and both with a strong vein of poetic vision.

In particular, I like evocative phrases such as "silver chill of snowy yesteryears" or, "soul perceives by eye, sees by ear, hears by taste." The apposite metaphors of "Soul" give it an almost Oriental starkness and deceptive simplicity.

I could point the reader to many more poems, and must admit to being an admirer of Curzon! As a late flowerer myself, in the shadow of my father, Dylan Thomas, I feel a sympathy with his late, but not *too* late, artistic flowering.

This resulting collection of poems from G. Curzon, entitled *TRINERGY*, may, perhaps, also refer to the three Ages of Man, and I am sure will be enjoyed by those of all ages. It is with enthusiasm I wish this poet a deserving success with this, his first volume, and others in the future.

Aeronwy Thomas-Ellis
New Malden, Surrey

A FEW WORDS

IMAGES SHATTER FORTH like orange California poppies in a green cut-glass bowl. Fragmentation seems pervasive in a divisive and divided world. Art, science and politics seem to show ever-increasing fragmentation and alienation. Yet man, aping God, tries to create order out of chaos.

I believe it is the prime function of the truly creative human to work towards wholeness and wholesomeness. Scientists and philosophers have used poetic metaphors to express the inexpressible, to accommodate ideas to language and language to thought. It may be, then, that the poet might be best equipped to handle notions of an all-pervasive sense of order in our small blue globe and in this vast universe.

I conceive the notion of *TRINERGY* as some sort of poetic force which is in Nature and the Universe and ties all together into an encompassing whole, no matter how disparate or fragmented the parts may seem to be.

Very much like magnetism, which seems to exist between two poles or gravity which seems to exist between bodies, or electricity, which seems to exist between two particles, and all of which seem to involve some sort of force, or energy greater than two alone, I came up some years ago with the notion of *TRINERGY*. I began to think of it as a *third* force emanating from the interplay of pairs, couples of ideas, facts, people, places, things or circumstances.

Reduced to human dimensions *TRINERGY* involves the spark between man and woman in all their complexities, and, with God, implicates the mystery of Trinity, and inspires one poet to speak of the three Ages of Man. It may also be reduced to Emily Dickinson's bee, flower and field of clover.

The poems are lyric, metaphysic and narrative. The artwork is complementary, serving a sense of transcendence. My poems are infused with notions derived from Einstein, Teilhard de Chardin, Bohr, and other creative scientists and poets. Many are embued with my own strong sense of the presence of God.

I name these three books *anthologies*, wreaths of flowers:

      I.   American Anthology
      II. Chicago Memories
      III. California and Beyond

All are trinergistic.

I leave it to mathematicians, physicists and philosophers — and other poets, to work out their own equations, arguments and metaphors. I offer you the metaphor of $TRINERGY$ as a possible think-link which may help unify men and women, their arts and sciences with their destinies — and their God.

BOOK I

AN AMERICAN ANTHOLOGY

EDUARDO DA SILVA

O God! I thought I'd died twice, when I heard the news
That Richard Burton had died. At fifty-eight yet, and me
Pushing sixty-five and glad to be alive. Died, alived. Booze
Probably got to his brain. Still —

I teach at a small Community College, down the hill
From my place. I had a wife and a basketball team
Of sons. All gone. Wife gone. Me fending off chill
Of late evening down winds. Still, I love the steam

Of my hot-tub. But, more often than not I soak alone,
And leave my seven cats to forage. I have always said
That man must make acommodation. I do my own.
Now, I must make syllabi for classes I dread.

Chicanos from my valley may just dig the words
That Burton told so well. "What a piece of work is man.
How noble in reason! How infinite in faculties!" Birds
Do it better. At least they twitter, but me, a sham.

O God! From desert, sandy, dry acre lot, my last place,
I look outside and see mountains and read my Shakespeare.
"In action how like angel! In apprehension, how like a god."
So, for me not so much quintessence of dust, but measure.

Accommodation. Well, it's served me until now.
I really have to prepare my classes,
And feed my cats. And yet, for me, I'd like to know,
What is this "quintessence of dust?" Ashes?

When, younger than a chick, I entered the convent,
I read *The Lives of the Saints* and quailed
At the horrors of Nero who kicked
His pregnant wife to death
And to crosses nailed
Christians.

Well, it took me a while longer to reinvent
A better cell in which to dwell.
And my heart still flutters
At the injustice
Of it all.

Now, older than the present Pope, I circumvent
The darkened spaces in my soul.
While my spirit is yet sorely afflicted
My soul flies, released on the wings of the dove.

DICK JOHNSON

Well, this is the way it was in Ngam Kuy.
We were on a sweep.
(To laymen — search and destroy.)
Ngam Kuy was a little mountain village,
Built by local tribesmen, proud people,
Hanging on to their highland home.

Actually, the village was full of crap,
And the shanty shacks
Full of women and kids at pap.
Mosta the men had took off, packs
And all, into the jungle.
And we was all set to rumble.

Those folk sure as hell din't know
'Bout the fire and flames
Our battalion was goin' to throw.
Then Leroy drug this Gook outa her shack.
She musta been fifteen or so.
Said, "I'm gonna get this baby on her back."

I dunno what come over me,
But there was this big, black buck,
So-called ol'buddy of mine.
I took out my forty five, put it on cock,
Said, "Do it man an' I'll blow your Goddam'
Head off."

Dunno why I said it. Twenty then,
Forty now. But I went wild.
Well, Leroy got mad, slapped the child.
Went off.
We thought we lived for what we died for.
But, looking back, I wonder.

Jesus Christ, do I ever wonder.

There's no looking back for *me!*
There's always the opportune moment
For the ultimate academician.

When to seize a scholar's certainty,
And devise a simple torment
For some dumb rhetorician

In my department, is my pleasure.
Ford Maddox Ford was my mentor;
His *Good Soldier* mine own measure.

Outstanding teacher I! I treasure
Students of the female variety.
(Tormenter I, of three wives —)

"Volcanic," my detractors say I am.
Little can they fathom contrariety
Of those whose private hells are lives

So unlike mine. Those who dwell ever
In the present tense, immense,
Can never lead a life intense

As mine, paradigm of professors.
Ever-seeking, ever consumptive,
I feast on presumptive confessors.

Captain Ashburn led a fulsome life,
And yet, most unholy. My last wife
Said that I lived mine most wholly.

My Ma was a waitress in Chicago
At the World's Fair in thirty-three.
My Dad, so she said, was a hero
In the CPD where he, believe me,
Was a cop on the vice-squad and
Arrested Sally Rand once for fans
In the air instead of on her snatch.
That's what Ma said — years ago.

I could hardly believe nothing Ma
Said. She had so many men friends
And three husbands. I ain't for sure
Which one was really my Dad. It tends
To make a good story, though, and I
Was always one for a good story, though
Ma used to call them lies.
                              My friends
Were mostly guys and gals my Ma knew. . .

I had an older sister, Kate, but she don't
Have much to do with me. Anyhow, Ma
Split from McCann, took me and Kate
On the Greyhound bus to LA where Ma
Got work in a defense plant. This was
A real exciting time. But I won't go into
Details.
         But, when I was seventeen I found
I had more going for me than my red hair.

One of them Marine cowboys told me I had
More between my legs than a horse. So I
S'pose I got on to be a hustler, though Dad
Sure as shit would've disapproved. I, rustler,
Looking back, wonder. Who's the hustled?
Who's the hustler?

For me life has been *nakhes und tsimmes*.
My parents came from the Ukraine
To escape the pogroms. Papa changed
The family name from Nudelman to Nadel.
Better he should have changed it to 'Ness,'
Like the monster, or some other name
Slightly more goyish. To make up his mind
He couldn't. To send me, Nate, the oldest,
To college, was his fondest wish. I tried.

When I was just twenty, he died, deranged,
In Mt. Sinai Hospital. The tumor on his brain
Affected his mind. My mother, Shirley, cried.

New York! - City College was now only a dream.
At business I wasn't much good. Garments
Held for me only smell of Papa's sweatshop.
Against advice I married a *shikseh*. *Goyim!*

Emily had class, was good in the kitchen,
If not in bed. We had no children. I came
To feel it was her fault, not mine. When
I got a young Puerto Rican immigrant
Pregnant, it was a hassle. So, what to do?

Palm Springs! California! From cutting cloth
To serving broth! So, we closed a series
Of restaurants, the last named Nate Badrigian.
Me with my nose! Em got depressed, went
To a shrink, decisive as always. For me decision
Not made is decision. So! I'm not Armenian!

At this stage in my life, with Em on her encounter
Group, maybe I'll just go to Temple next *shabbes*,
But, then again. . .

GLABRA CARPENTER

We met each other coming across the parking lot
Outside a restaurant in Santa Barbara.
We hugged. It was a simple moment. No plot.
He, so properly, introduced me to Mara,
His wife, Glenda, his sister-in-law,
And Jarl, his sister-in-law's husband.

We made small talk. It had begun to rain.
Look, I've been involved in professional
Counselling, Kräftig Gefühl, with umlauts
Yet, weeping on shoulders, the whole bit!
He admired my dress, the way it fit!
I was simply looking for another place
To live, another house. What a bucket!

So, what's another client? I need an agent.
The rain came down harder. So we went.
I got in my van, he and three into rain.
Me? Professional counsellor! What a crock!
He? Big head, small brains, nice jock.

MARIA HERNANDEZ

May Mary, Mother of God, help me!
I went to bed with this man. He
Tol' me his wife, Em, hated him.
I loved Nate. He is a good man. He
Loved me, I loved him. I sewed
For him in his shop on Seventh
Avenue. Okay, I got laid. De nada.

In Puerto Rico there is a saying
That for a man any a hole will do.
I went to confession. Father Kreuz,
Forgave me my sin. I told him a Jew
Did it. He tol' me to pray.

Now, Nate has closed his store
He don't need me anymore. He is
Going to Palm Springs, with Em.
I have sister in Indio. She is
Married up with a Mexican.
I hope they will love my Jew niño.

RHONDA WEAVER

My maiden name was Madigan. John,
The Weaver part of me, divorced me.
His paramour — how old-fashioned!
Was his secretary in the Art Depart-
ment. He later became a Dean! On
The occasion of my fiftieth birthday
I bought a loom.
Now there are those beautiful intimacies —
There are those betwixts and betweens —
There are certain mellownesses of yarns —
And small uprisings.

When I look at my small contexts
Of woof and warp, when I plect
Weaves of waves and rip unruly
Threads of desire, I see my sex
In a new view. No longer asunder,
I can afford to plunder young men.

Carl is my hair-dresser. I wonder
If he, at twenty four, will ever come
To grips with my need to grasp.
For me to insert my lock in his hasp
Is mightiness. Still, he tints, combs
And strokes my hair, and calls me
Clytemnestra! What a puppy! The fool!

My great grandmother was born a slave.
Her name was Ella Mae. Grampa Steele
Told me once Ella Mae was bought for
Breeding purposes. Now I begin to feel
His long-smouldering rage. He gave
Me the urge to achieve and do and be real.

Maybe, for me, this was not enough. I
Needed to make and build. So I took
Martin's last name as one of mine. I
Shook at the doors of Alabama, then I
Was finally permitted to enter. Now I
Am an architect, designer of dreams.

No, I don't build no more. I teach.
When I got this job at the University
I attended a new faculty party. Each
Novice played the game. A stupid honkie
Smilingly asked me if I was to teach
Ethnic studies. I felt the old rage in me.

That's what one eighth white blood
Has done for this tough stud!

THELMA BOLES

My arthritis has been acting up
And now that Charles is gone
There's only my one son, Bud
Left, and he ain't much help,
Being as how he's mostly on
Medication at the Vet's for
Cancer. Got it in Viet Nam
From Agent Orange, the Doc
Said. Well, after my oldest son,
Rick passed on suddenly, and
Left a wife and two kids, and
My cousins in Kansas are on
In years, there's no one much
Left.

I sure wish the grandchildren would
Take time to write me now and then.
But, I guess they're too busy. Young
People don't think, I guess. Yet when
I was up and around and not hung
Up with doctoring, I allus wrote.
Well, Christmas is comin' on . . . .

I am a Southern gentleman, born
and raised in Lexington, Kentucky
where good horses and fried chicken come
from

My Mama always told me to respect
women, even Blacks, and I suspect,
corn liquor, taxes, and the Methodist
form

Of religion. But even a silly subject
like old faith loses some respect
when put to the test of the funny
farm.

For Christian love runneth over,
and here I stand deprecating myself
because I am not a Harvard professor,
or whatever.

I teach in a big department in a big
University in a big State and I
have principles, though some say I
haven't.

No one gives me a pat on the back —
a stab, maybe, — in the hall, a black
ball, a nastiness, an ugliness.
Hell!

Southern gentleman? Son, I've
learned to curb my loquacity.
Don't force me to examine my drive.
I might

Just start to examine yours! Don't attack
my *amour propre*, for you get at the kernel
of my being. Colonel Sanders' chickens might
fight back

2

At your attempts at skewering. You shaft
energy on arrows. Barrows of poultry
waste are expended on paltry
insight.

I am a Southern gentleman! I look
in my mirror and see true nobility.
I am not like my Arkansas cousin, Bob,
the snob.

He fancies *he's* a Southern gentleman,
yet he uses "ain't" in his versions
of regional dialect. He, too is pissing,
the slob,

On himself, yet he fancies himself
a scholar. Yankee Emily said the soul
selects its own society. What pelf!
Good God!

I prize my privacy. I don't always
answer my phone. I prefer to be alone.
I am sick and I drink. But I've bought
a plot.

I am a true Southern gentleman.

Since Mabel's gone I watch TV more.
We used to walk along the bluff each
Day and watch the gulls along the shore,
But, she's gone now. I don't drink much,
But I'll be dammed if these videos
Won't drive me to the bottle. I watched
This gal with a square mouth froze
In a perpetual sneer and hair like a thatched
Roof we once saw in England. She looked
Like a skinned frog in her black pants
And never once did she smile. She shook
Her head real mean like, and I never did
Get the words she said. She never did dance
But pranced 'round like Mussolini. Goddam!
What a sight! No man in his right mind
Would have any truck with a witch
Like that! Now, my Mabel. . . . Well, like
I said, she's gone now. Guess I'll watch
Ted Koppel. . .

MARK ANTHONY DEXTER, POET

There seems to be some common culprit
Indian in my strange word wanderings. It
Might be attributed to my love of Mother.

She is now buried in a cask of rum on
A reservation in the State of Washington.
I really do not know what I have done

To deserve the womb that I was born from.
Next my wigwam were the Wahkiakum,
Just another Indian tribe, love "other."

My strange range might be attributed to
My love of "other," mother. Like Escher,
Picture poems turn back one and one, two.

Like strictures of long-lost loneliness
And apparitions and partitions high blown
In lone Yakima skies, which slowly dress

In lunar yardage, and seem to be from moon
Of gray graces and high towers where plume
Of Mount St. Helen's descends on

One's own Klickitat backyard, words and
Verse demand payment in cash, not ash,
And verbal tumulus is reckoned in Krugerrand.

ETTA GOLDING STERN

a. k. a. Ms Lit

I sing for you —
I give to you my voice —
I live for you, rejoice —
In all that belongs to you
and me —
The upthrusting mountain —
The female surge of sea.

I sing! I cry! I weep with the wave,
The pregnant curl which inturning,
In foam impregnates
My wanton wasteland
And spends itself on sea-sand,
As, sucked in, drawn down,
It dissipates itself, all in all.

I need a man, a kind man,
An ever-loving, warm man
To hear my trembling cry, and share
With me my fear of world and ware,
Of toil and trade, of gut and blade.
I need that strong-shouldered one,
That stormy, unbegotten son
Who will ever love me and mine —
Enough to match my pains,
Enough to unlatch my chains.

IDA NUDEL

I ache for you, Ida Nudel.
You've known the icy hell
of Siberia.

For you I pray. I tell
In words of your cold cell,
O Miseria!

You want to live — rebel,
And die in Israel —
O *Refusenik!*

For you no Christian bell
I ring. A miracle
For you I seek.

My headsman, Dr. Schwarzweiss, gives with advice —
Not always good, but, with a question, adequate.
For fifty dollars a half hour I should wait
For his advice to sink in? Better I should be
Drinking! Or fooling around? Still, it could be a vice.
Alcohol distilled from the grape makes brandy,
And with that I am not so handy. Leads to lethargy.
Schwarzweiss advises, "Have you tried Maneschewitz?"
"No!" — "Yes!" — I stutter. For me, too sweet. *Toute suite!*

He pushes me toward the couch with three prods and a punch.
At twenty comes the crisis of identity?
At forty comes the crisis of maturity?
At sixty comes the crisis of senility?
Other words I sense for crises are age and death. A bunch
Of crap! I worry about taxes and — bitterly, plots,
And that's what takes my breath away — literally —
Not to be confused with too many cigarettes —
Late in life come a series of vignettes —

Cut, like scenes from a movie projector run backwards
Like Hebrew. I think my sixty crisis came at six
When I learned Lennie Adelman had choked to death
On a wiener, a Kosher one at that! I held my breath.
My forty crisis came at twenty and stayed like a plague
For plenty years until the last of the holocaust corpses
Were buried or burnt like a smoldering coal in my soul.
Now, past sixty, I face my indentity of twenty.
An old friend wants to know if mark the High Holidays.

Perplexed, I ask Schwarzweiss. Like any good shrink
He answers a question with a question, a shrug and a wink
Of his rheumy eye, "What's a Jew?"
For fifty dollars a half hour I should wait
For an answer? Better, I should call Pope John Paul's beanie
A *yarmakah* and trade in my old tuxedo for a *tallis*.
The God of Abraham and Isaac and Jacob was a meanie!
Or maybe the ancient prophets got his message crossed.
"How odd of God to choose the Jews!" I feel like Alice

In Wonderland! I ask my learned *gonif* if he has ever felt
Frustrated. "Frustrated! What do you mean by frustrated?"
Always the question! Like dear Gertrude Stein
On her deathbed asking, "What's the answer?" Mine
Are her final words, "What's the question?" I guess I rated
Schwarzweiss as a psychiatrist with an identity crisis,
Because he asked me last session "Who do *you* think I am?"
Always the question! "Am I your friend?" Well, ice is
On my tongue as I reply, "Nu! So you are the King of Siam?"

For once Dr. Mastermind surprises me with an answer.
"You do not need me any more." Perfect iambic tetrameter!
"My son David, the youngest one, needs a class in Lit. . ."
Always the hint of the question! And, guess who is "It!"

AROUND THE BEND

Whenever I am asked to quote a line
Of poetry I say, "I think that I
Shall never see a poem lovely
As a tree." And, if pressed, I
Go on to the line about the breast.

Poems today are not wrung in rhyme
Or meter —
And that may just go with salt-petre.
What makes a poet rise above mere
Statement? Poem, a casement,

Through which man views his state
As in a Breughel painting, or is it more?
Round the bend — for sure......
Ecdysiasts contemplate navels of
Eternity, and young men lather. Small

Trees grow in infinitudes on longbeaches,
To where the horizon tilts up and reveals
Skirts and stockings of mocking demons.
Steamboat! I hear your horn around the bend,
Forlorn on the banks of the ol' Missouri.

What do canal boats answer in Amsterdam?
People particulate short odysseys, and
It is the brave man who dares tell them
The King has no clothes on. Poor old Priam!
Except tellum, dance goes round and round.

We yell and jump and dance and prance.
We leap through hoop and take the lance
Between our ribs while we ask and answer,
Seek the teaser, hump the chancer —
Always following the programmed script.

Round the bend for sure are we —
Figure eights contemplate eternity
Like a showering down of dried leaves
Covering corpse of what might have been.
So, take no solace, then. How archaic

Statement that. Not non-plussed, ache
Hurts. We all know that. So, shall we all
Compare our aches? Is that what it takes?
Or, shall we all go 'round the bend —
Together?

According to a psychiatrist from UCLA, reported today
By the Associated Press, people like Churchill
And Handel were mad.

Dr. Jamison said she hopes her study will help lay
People appreciate the positive side of ill
Artists, and sad

To say, poets and writers and painters and members
Of Britain's Royal Academy. I hope she will
Include the bad

Folks like me, and will perhaps remember
That there's a certain irrationality still
To art. I'm glad.

EPITAPH

Dying is for the living —
Death is but beginning —
My faith is my freight —
Unlatched is the gate.

God's wonders there are —
Beyond each distant star —
Space is time's membrane —
For Heaven, mere lane.

Should those who remain —
Wish to maintain —
Memories of a man —
Let them look up and scan.

For me let them build —
A good, sturdy bench —
Of wood un-milled —
Or of stone, and drench

It with a lively libation —
Of sea water and wine —
And let them write thereon —
A suitable inscription.

BOOK 2

CHICAGO MEMORIES

COMING OF AGE IN CHICAGO

Polyglot town! "That toddlin' town, (Capone spent) —
Stop puttin' it down!" Or so the words went —
Bent early on, I learned to decipher Hebrew —
KOSHER writ large on chicken shop windows
Where, in the back the *schicket* slit white necks.

Then there was the famous Polish restaurant —
Kuchnia domowa — "home cooking" it boasted
And the smells of Kosher chickens roasted
Blended with formaldehyde fumes from
The Polish underaking parlor — *Balsamator*.

Milwaukee Avenue's long Northwest finger
Prodded neighborhoods into action with red
And yellow street cars whose trolleys we used
To disengage on Halloween before a trick in bed
With a Black in a flat on Lake Sreet over the El.

Then! The smell! The smell of the wodka at Lenards,
Where first I crunched caviar and the *kielbbasa*
Was the specialty of the house, and Casimir hit
Hammers on strings and we polkaed, and peed
From the *pivo!* Tak! One, two, three — hop!

And Halina Wrobleska called me *kochanie*
And I did not know what it meant until Ignaz
Told me in the toilet, "Sweetheart!" And, yeah
Dai me buzshe, meant, "Give me a kiss!" As
We teetered toward trolley, we pissed our youth away.

Christmasses came, Hannukahs, too. New Year's Eves
We'd eat pickled herring and throw darts at Hitler's
Face on Bund posters. Christian and Jew, we knew
The brew that was brewing — yet like the leaves
That fell that Autumn, we settled into spittle.

We spat at Hitler. We spat at Tojo. We spat at —
Then the world fell in. Warsaw, ghettoes and ovens
Melted in blood — and schickets and chickens meant
Nothing at all, at all. *BOG!* The Polacki priests
Cried over candles. *ADONAI!* Cried the Jews . . .

But it was no use, no use. *Dziennik Chicagoski*
Reported the news, and so did the Chicago Tribune
And the Daily News — and the Jewish Daily Forward,
And — it was all the same. The bombers came in tune
With the early Sunday sun and then we were at war. . .

It may be it was then we came of age. After the rage,
After the flags, the bunting, the speeches, the spit,
After marching away, casualty lists on each front page.
It was all the same, then. It is all the same again. Shit!
And a Polack sits on the throne of Peter! *Shalom!*

Sen-Sen scented Dillinger
walked out of the Biograph
near North Clark & Fullerton
that hot night in Chicago
and a Lady in Red was under his arm.

She was not Evelyn Frechette
with whom he had slept
in that wet Wisconsin lodge
with stagheads on the walls.

The Lady in Red, late papers said,
was Rumanian. A new love?
A whore, they said.
Glorious in red, swaying in sweet
swill of his aura, she held his waist.

Orange squad cars used to whine
on Chicago's streets.
This one, though, golding through green,
unpeeled plain-clothed police.
While Dillinger strolled alleywards
the Lady lagged to brush a lash.

Suddenly at alley all
converged in urgency of time.
Police shots glared in vollied flood
and Dillinger fell, losing pulse
in warm slosh of spurting blood.

There was a telephone pole
at his felt-hatless head,
and it stretched up into the dark...
cross-bars latched with black
wires, crossed and double-crossed.

Next morning
I watched still milling people
in the red brick alley,
and there were those there
obscenely wiping the red bricks
with, and
daubing their spit-wet white
handkerchiefs
in Dillinger's drying blood.

South on State Street beyond Van Buren,
Tawdrier progessively toward Congress,
Past hallway walk-ups smelling of urine,
Go high school boys on rake's progress.

St. Pat's seniors cajole the Sally Anns
With tales of sin and drink, and plans
For complete conversion on the spot —
But blue-bonneted brigade see no plot.

Kenneth Casey confesses sins uncommited.
He gets one more brass Army play.
When late crowd's lust permitted
He'd regale with tales of unrequited lay.

With upstairs whores in windows bent
On hearing his erotic tales, intent
Is Ken on plea for tromboned blessing.
Later, before dawn Mass, he's confessing.

WABASH AVENUE

Under the El, east of State Street,
Loop's nondescript edge, with a fleet
Of bars, always under gloom,
Though sunlight flickered through —
Gradually unravelled.

In roar and crash of trains and trolleys,
Pigeons, perch disturbed, flew in volleys
And whitened second floor entrances —
Carson, Pirie, Scotts, Marshall Fields's
Quick! On Lake Street curve, rail yields.

Ties and tracks splinter —
As if in tangled dreams —
Angel wings flicker —
Above the blood and screams.

Were You there watching with me? Were You
On the platform when the El trains crashed?
Or were You down on the red bricks
When life dripped down on Wabash Avenue?

It was in Garfield Park I had lessons
On how to drive. Thirty-six Essex,
Axe to root, Chicago policeman tried
To teach me how to start and go, to turn
And brake, come back again and park.
Like untracked trolley, I, wheeling wide,
Lurched car over curb, my youth astride,
And wound up in a clump of tamarack.

It was in Garfield Park, I, confession's
Long line done, penance said, would go
On my way to the show — talking pictures —
Saturday matinee, (A walk through the Park!)
And watch, entranced, as theater organ
Would slowly rise up from down below,
And a Klieg would play on Maestro Mark
Hammond. (Or was that the name of his organ?)

It was in Garfield Park I had sessions
In botany (and biology) in the Conservatory
With a female graduate student from the University
Of Chicago. She was entranced with plants
And pants, pistils and anthers, anthuriums.
Class gone, she asked to stay to wander
Under palms, fondling foliage and diversity.
I learned to drive behind Palm House steam pipes.

It was in Garfield Park, I, transgressions
Marked amidst banana plants, philodendron,
Steam pipes' winter hiss, learned discretions
Of driving and mating. City forest glade gone
Now, except in memory. Magic of Park freshens
Bittersweetnesses of youth and bush, cretonne
Of priapismic gardens. Like most possessions,
Those first acquired, last thrown away — anon!

I'll never forget that torrid day
When the heat, like a sauna, lay
Heavy over Chicago and Eddie and I
Had this Summer job on the NYA. My
Job was to help Eddie paint the hall
Ceiling in the gym. We'd done the wall,
Moved the ladders, took off our shirts,
And finally our pants. Down to shorts
We painted the afternoon heat. Two skirts
Appeared, stood under ladders. All sorts
Of thoughts steamed through my head.
The girls were Italian, sisters; black
Hair, very pretty. I was blonde, so was Ed,
Blue-eyed, too. I English, he Polack.

Le due Italiani were evidently taken
With Eddie and me. Up from the floor
They gazed with hot eyes. Somewhat shaken
From the heat and the height, muscles sore,
We straddled the ladders. Then, with a smirk,
Ed whispered to me that the girls could see
Right up our shorts. Pretending to work
On the spills, I clambered down, took a look
Up. Ed was right. I could see to his groin.
Exhibitionistic Polack I thought! Rules of Book
Forbade indecent display, and eyes could not join
In sin, much less thighs. Later, after dates
And wine, I wondered whose thoughts
Were most sinful, the sisters' or mine!

It was a moon away — the land of Black,
Of whores and pimps and prostitutes,
And yet it was the very urgent lack
Of egress that compelled White substitutes.

One day I met Cassandra at the House
Of Hospitality sweet Dorothy
Got off South Side. Dear Day, Lord's spouse!
And there it all began, the sympathy.

And there came unravelled skeins of genes.
I came to love black skin, cocoa, coffee,
Caramel, *cafe au lait*, and creams
Of cinnamon, toast and toffee.

I loved the dance, the prance, the jut,
The strut, the arrogance, the ambience,
Boys' well marbled muscles, their flood
Of male, Cassandra's flamboyance.

Soul's sympathy's no substitute for love.
Too late I came to know a sorry fact
That teen-age love was bound by rules above,
That I was White and she was Black.

My invitation to her Senior Prom
At St. Elizabeth's Black Senior High
Was foreseen. A cream! A coming from!
No hope proffered. Crass culprit I.

"You'll be an oyster in a bed of coal,"
Sister Agnes said. I sweat, prayed, bled, died.
And wondered if through sex I'd lose my soul,
Or if, perchance, by race I might be fried.

And so it came to pass, while fondling Cass,
Enjoying tits and ass, without remorse
I told a lie. "June ten, I got to go to Mass.
My Grandma died. Late wake, of course."

Remorse. Yubetcha. Evennow. Remorse.
I wonder who she took? A Black, I guess — —

I still remember those great
Porticos. I forget now, Doric
Or Corinthian. It was the fate,
Once yearly, that metaphoric

Best of public versus Catholic
High-school foot-ball teams
Would vie for glory. Terrific
Contests those. Now it seems

So very far away.
They ran, they won,
They lost. One day
For them in the sun.

O, dear boys, could stone
Columns tell of death
Before time, of lone
Lives lost, of one last breath?

MADISON AND KEDZIE

Dear Bob: Thanks for your letter. I had
No idea you grew up on the West Side.
The year you were born we lived at
2741 Jackson Boulevard. The old place
Is still there, yellow brick, now all
Black with a neon sign outside. Then
We moved to Mrs. Mc Kenna's rooming house
At 3314 Monroe. She had two sons, Pat
And Mike. We used to go to the movies at
The Kedzie Annex. Sometimes we would
Sneak in to the Kedzie Theater to watch
The plays. They were all Yiddish. Nate
Cohen would rent movies to the Catholic
School — Our Lady of Sorrows. During Lent
He would rent "The King of Kings." The nun
Who ran the projector also ran the candy
Shop in the basement of the School. I won
Candy bars on penny chocolate mints. White
Was a loser. Chocolate center, a winner.

The red brick school is gone. The red brick
Streets are gone. The street cars are gone.
Black asphalt now, smooth and slick.
Chocolate center there now.
                              Bob, keep on
Writing me about Chicago. I'll be quick
To reply, Yours —

The Chicago, Aurora and Elgin ran
Big red cars west above Van Buren
On the El tracks until Oak Park,
Where the trains came down on
The ground. Rocketing after dark,
The lights went out whenever break
In third rail broke flow of spark
To electric motor.

What excitement for a young lad
Bound for Christmas at Gramps!
Crossing bells ding-aling-alinged
Approaching quick crossing. Lamps
Flicked out and ding-a-lings had
Slower fling snowy roads lept.
Brief black brought quick glimpse
Of far and near Holiday trees lit.

Past Batavia Junction, one car left,
Others on way to Geneva and Elgin.
One last car past Aunt Mayme's, on
Past Reuland's farm where agents
Shot Bill over still full of bootleg gin
Last hot August. Bitter cold now,
Window frost-glazed, except where
I'd scratched a spy-hole in the rime.

Aurora Avenue! Last lights flicker
As iron runner leaves third rail,
Uncle Nick waiting in '31 Buick
Touring sedan. Lone car leaves trail
Of electric sparks on way down Fox
River to end of line. Yet to go — trek
Up Pigeon Hill, wheels acrunchin' snow
To Grampa's house and warm bunk.

Family voices drift up from kitchen
Below through heat grill. Poker game
Played with chips stored in mop-wax
Pail. "Gimme three!" "Pass!" "Check!"
"Bet five!" "Raise!" "Call!" "Full house!"
"Hear about the Zimmerman's kid? In
The Beacon News today. Slipped on
The ice, fell on the third rail. . . . . ."

Mrs. Mc Kenna loved the Sheenie Market.
The best day to shop was Sunday.
The best time was after last Mass.
And, after all, shoppin' wasn't work
Though sellin' was, accordin' to Father Ryan.
She'd get son Mike, Mom and me on the run
To the Madison street-car. Off at Halsted
We'd throng our way to Maxwell Street.

Mike and I took in the sights and smells
Of strange sausages and stranger fish.
While Mrs Mac and Mom haggled, we'd
Try to swipe a peach or plum. I wish
I knew who told us the lie it wasn't wrong
To steal from a Jew. Well, then no heed.
Carts and barrows, dirty gutters — greed
Of merchants, greed of buyers had a fun day.

Worst of my moments were upstairs
Clothes rooms where Mike and I were
Fitted with knickers and jackets! Airs
Of astonishment over the prices! A hand
On the ass, a hand on the crotch — All
The while wheedling, all the while smiles.
Once I got bought a real red, artificial
Rubber raincoat. I hated it. It developed tears.

Mike and I were hard on clothes. All us boys
Were hard on clothes, both Jews and goys.
"Izzie, Ikie, Jakie, Sam! We're the boys
Who eat no ham!" "Paddie, Mikie, Shakey,
Art! We're the boys from Sacred Heart!"
Maybe it was in Maxwell Street I learned
Who had the last laugh. There, in the mart
Of long gone Sundays lessons were earned.

OUR LADY OF SORROWS

Twin towered temple to the faithful
Still stands century safe but with
Cracks in the plaster. Old red school
Bricks across Albany, dead monolith.

But, in 1927! Gangster funeral brought
Al Capone into the sacristy where he
Gave each impounded altar boy a dollar
After requiem high Mass.

                                    I still see
The snow furrowed along Jackson, where
Once I found a dollar bill! Wet, but still
A dollar bill, and Sister sold chances
In the candy store. A choc center will

Get a kid a candy bar, and I wondered
Whether Sister Henrietta had satin
Hair under coif, and Brother Blundert
Taught us how to respond in Latin.

Fortitudo mea — came out forty-two
Tomatoes. And the men trailing behind
The casket along the marble paid due
Respect, fedoras in hand, with a kind

Of holiness there amidst the candles.
*Dies irae, dies illa . . . Solvet saeclum
In favilla.* Vanilla ice-cream, handles
On casket, dollar bills, chewing gum.

*Sancta Maria, Sancta Dei Genetrix,
Sancta Virgo virginem,* from thy altar,
Ora pro nobis! Sanctus Deus Mix
Master, pray for us! For we falter.

Always thought how improbable
A name was Wacker!
Sunny side of the Tribune Tower,
Downline from the Palmolive Beacon
Was Millie's. She was able
To run her small place an hour
Or two a day, eleven to one,
Specializing in liver and onions,
With generous garnish of bacon.

Lace curtains on sliding brass rings
Hid hurried ad-men from
Batton, Barton, Durstine and Osborn
And battered writers from
Colonel McCormick's stable.
For fifty cents one ate well. A horn
Of plenty was Millie's table
On Wacker! Funny name, Wacker!

MARSHALL FIELD'S BASEMENTS

Marshall Field's famous Department Store
Occupied one square block in Chicago's Loop
And part of another.

The other, the Men's Store was not my terrain.
Mine was meeting Momma
In the basement, Ladies Hosiery, Section 210,
Just before closing time.

Registers counted, cash in bag turned in
To massive, diagonal wire-braced teller in concrete,
One more basement down below,
We went to the lockers, retrieved purse, coat, galoshes.

Still, one more basement down was the machinery
That made it all work.
I never saw the turbines, the motors, the heat.
But, back up, once more to the teller,
This time the payer.
Brown paper envelope, two fives and a two
For forty-eight hours.

Marshall Field was a friend of Levi Z. Leiter.
Made their way into England
Founding department stores.
Levi's daughter, Mary, married a Lord of the Realm.

But, that was some time before
Marshall Field's had more than one basement.

Early on I had graduated
From long brown stockings
Held up by plus-fours
Buttoned below the knees
To long pants and socks
Held up by garters cinched
Around and above the calves.

It was in Orchestra Hall
On Michigan Boulevard
After a solo performance
By Lawrence Tibbett that
My right garter got all
Unhooked as we walked out
To "A Serenade for Strings."

Sock ankle sagging, Paris
Garter dragged up aisle like
Ball on chain-gang member.
Betty pretended not to notice
But I knew she saw my shame.
I've never cared much for
Unadulterated suites for strings.

RIVERVIEW PARK

That last hot Summer before the
War, when it became unpopular
To do so, the Bund held *Hochfest*
At Riverview Park, raffled off
Smoked German eels, stiff
As riding crops, and sang *Horst
Wessel Lied.. "Die Fähne hoch,
Die Reihe dicht geschlossen."*

Bob Marciewicz and I would swipe
Bottles of Löwenbrau München
And watch German shepherd dogs
Draw blood from pigs ripe
For slaughter. After lunching
On stolen *wurst*, we'd stand
On Belmont Bridge for hours
And count the condoms afloat
Down Chicago's North Branch.

Simple math showed that rate
And frequency of coition on
The Northwest side was great
Enough for the US to win a war,
We figured. Later, lying on bank,
Darkness came, and we'd watch
The parachutes drop, and swig
The last of the stolen German beer.

THE ORIENTAL

I remember Grandma used to take me
To matinees at the Oriental Theater.
In the lobby was a big, black, grand piano
That used to play all by itself. We would
Watch the keys move mysteriously
Up and down as it played "Nola."
But there was no place to put a roll in.

We would climb the big staircase
To the black balcony, take our seats
In the front row and watch the Klieg
Lights roll across the stage. After
The vaudeville show and talking picture
Grandma and I would leave and retrace
Our steps down the marble stairs
To where the big, black, grand piano
Was still playing. The keys still would
Be going up and down — mysteriously.

There was the Sky-ride astride
Twin towers called Amos and Andy
And Sally Rand and her famous fan
Dance which we youngsters heard
Only by rumor, and there was the Hall
Of Science, magic pavillion! We'd ride
On the street-cars from all over town
To see the sights and wonders. I can
Still remember the thrill of a ball
Peen hammer made of frozen mercury
With which one could drive a nail!

I can't recall the number of times
I went to that sacred shrine and
Soaked up the mysteries of Science.
There was one particularly nice man
Who'd give me specimens on microscope
Slides, and once loaned me two dimes
For a late evening snack, and last even
Paid my way home on the street-car
Because he lived in my neighborhood.
At his suggestion we took a short cut
Down an alley. Innocence of boyhood!
In darkness of shadows, I learned quick
That even a man of Science was not
To be trusted. So much for the packet
Of slides, lying broken on the brick
Of the alley and the rip in my jacket.

Ojibwa, wah! wah! was a nice tribe
Of Indians who lived near
The Pottawattomi in Illinois,
Kankakee. (The Beaujolais were indolent.)
Time well spent in frying skunk patch
Chicago shoot apparitions: Caesar,
Al Capone, Chavez, away, Bent
It now around with bring.

From Southwestamerican sand deserts
Strato liners arrive one by one in
Heathrow, O'Hare, London, Claridges
And that young Harrod's lady
Who just checked out my baggage
Planted maize in Peoria, and
Really, it doesn't matter,
"Thank you so veddy much!" Ta.

That winsome lass minus one
Has left Winnebago territory
To seek Shoshone in London
Where Meg, Phil and Charlie boy
Had decided to go to Wiesbaden
By way of Urbana to visit the Pope
On the very same day the soap
Opera was being performed in Beijing
By a troupe of well-muscled Navaho
Under the guise of sausages from
Iran and hostages from Canton.

In, in the din, in inauguration opera
Wise brokers sighed with relief
At the release of Pottawattomies
After the demise of the Shah of Iran,
And the Indian lass who advertizes
Mazola on TV turns out to be
An Ashkenazi from Tel Aviv - (receive),
Who practices Zen while reciting
"*Baruch, Adonai, Elohenu,*" Torah on
The Johnny Carson Show from Washingon.

Still, Ronald, middle name Western
Celluloid cowboy, can't distinguish
Arapahoe from Cherokee, Sauk from Sioux,
Or extinguish in his aging loins
Humorem libidinis. He veddy true blue.
Oh well, folks, it really doesn't
Matter. Just take the Disney cruise
Down the tesselated stars on Holly-
Wood Boulevard and look for cracks
In the terrazzo. Wear the drag hat
Of the mad hatter, or feathers, yet.

Give a tea party in midst of the runway.
Faith of our fathers know! Hopi know!
Ojibwa wait, as always, for the chief
To die. Shoshone know, Capone know!
Indians no lie. They lie in wait in Kuwait.

Great!

IN MEMORIAM

A Transition

KENNETH REXROTH 1905 - 1982

We, who live after, hone and file fine feelings.
The invitation to a Russian Orthodox funeral mass
At Holy Trinity Cathedral on Van Ness
Went unheeded. Garden needed to be weeded.

Mariana, forgive me. Carol, forgive me. Unlike
Your father, your spouse, my words shrank.
From me, only a slight enconium, remembrance.
How unlike the times (o, the times!) in Bughouse
Square, Chicago — those primitive days, which,
Along with memories of Dorothy Day and other
Utter resemblances I wear, like old clothing.

Rexroth had a way with words. In late shade
Of eucalypt on Montecito patio, we drank tea.
Then, his words became paintings, paintings, words,
Those were his best days, those last days. We
Recalled blessed dissonances of the age.
Ken kept, like the old North Side water tower,
A Victorian high.

Long after Chicago words, Clark Street bars,
Bay animators, we laughed and wept. Ken
Acknowledged, after divisiveness, stars,
A secret hope for a fulmination of disasters.
His unorthodoxy spurred the University, then,
To let him go, and it was unachieved. Masters
And mimics heard.

For memories I fund him. No matter of tapes
Recorded on mutual trips to the High Sierra
When he talked knowledgeably about birds.
Old Chicago words were there. No matter me
Trying to locate the Thirties. To listen,
Early Eighties, always to listen to words.
And, last, the Church.

We throve on Gregorian. Taped Solesmes.
Attended lauds, then drove to the free beach,
(So unlike Oak Street) to view,
"Strong-ankled, sun-burned, almost naked,
The daughters of California." We each
Had different ways with words. Language
Lasts, voices heard.

His voice is now set in words. Concretized
I like to think that I knew him once.
Once in Chicago, once in California, many
Onces — in the beginning, in the end.

BOOK 3

CALIFORNIA and BEYOND

Syndrome: The act of running together.
A set of concurrent things.

What's so damned unusual
About a beach? Be it
Pacific, Dover, or Shell.
What the hell! So shall
All men die, each in his own
Private cell, who dare
Tell of private beaches.

Well, Plato, long ago, heard
The Phrygian bell, Circe's
Spell on Peloponesian strand.
So, what's so unseemly grand
About a beach? A string of sand
Keeping water from land? From
Afar single grains each make beach.

How can I say it, since I've said it?
Tide will swell and will not dwell,
Will withdraw, return and bring
To my soul slow ebb and flow
Of love. Yet, when by storm
Unleashed, exerts enough energy
To split rocks.

How can I love you more
Than on the beach? Where
The pelicans plunge, seals sun, and
Sea otters bash clam shells on
Their breasts with rocks, and
Sand fleas fly, and cars go by
On the freeway high above the shore.

No, this is not the Aegean!
But please don't be mean.
(I thot you'd like that line, love!)
I'll brush sand off sheets, kiss
Your salty feet and if our plumy
Strand suffice, I'll be there in a trice.
Our beach may be our private place,
And some, I think, do there embrace.
But when on us police lights do shine,
Good God, I'll take our downy bed any time!

The image flakes down, falters,
Then down-flames like
California poppies, alters,
Cracked in a green bowl.

Their petals are scattered
On the Mohave Desert,
Like a shattered dream
Come awake.

For some, dream began to go
On Ellis Island,
For others, San Ysidro.
For the rest, the land

Outlives the promise.
Dream frames of poppy pass.
O, no fine place is this,
Mere sherd-land, sharp as glass.

CALIFORNIA CHRISTMAS

There is no snowflake on this sunny beach.
The winds of winter do not often reach
This furrowed shore.

Yet, silver chill of snowy yester-years,
And children making festive rounds bring tears
To spill once more.

I'm never quite detached from past great joys
Of Christmases designed for girls and boys,
And sparkling trees.

Eyes' icy shards of glass do fall and flake,
And from a thousand prisms and mirrors take
Their Season's ease.

For those who flee from Shelley's beaten road
And find in love for more than one a code,
There's greater bliss.

There's no chained soul one dares call his own,
And then to make of life a double road, alone:
Mere artifice.

No! On my sandy beach I sit and gaze,
And think on Christmases in colder days
And, rue them not.

Christ's birth, a metaphor of sun and youth,
Delights my heart and shows a larger truth —
A love begot.

I seek among the ocean drills
On this sandy sea-shore
Microscopic animals
Bent on imminent thrills
Of living. And I explore.

I wonder with a new sense
Of bird wings' flight,
At that higher sight
As of ocean drained and depths
Laid bare — a new vision —

A precision of gold gone golder-
Of poppies blooming bolder —
Of bluets plumbing molten depths —
And loved one beside
Me. She teems inside

Like Pacific tide. Now to unfold,
Slow, like petalled bloom,
Her center fetalled spume.
Blest is one who wakes from
Such settled imagery

And quickly opens stuck eyes
To a new awareness. Dumb
Word that! A security of bees
In the hive is! But to be alive
Is throwing beeswax in the fire —

And destroying moulds of makers —
And seeing that violets are violetter —
And it is climbing tall green trees —
And letting lover's hands grope better —
And rhyming sea shells with pleas.

O, Sea song, which I now might sing,
Or even limn with scrawly pen,
Gently batter Heaven's house
And tell the angels, that, over them,
I must, naked, stride ahigh

Ever trying celestial portals —
Ever picking secret locks.

Slowly drying, like raisins in the sun,
they wait there in Wrinkle City —
a cemetery without a post-office, pun
makers say, trying to be witty.

Lemon light oozes through a pair
Of picture window drapes, hung
and drawn across to shade the glare.
Wasted hands wearing bands
of gold, unfold to show marks of time
and slowly grope for long-gone
grandchildren.

Golden anniversary portraits sit there
on the unused electric chord-organ
whose cord is not plugged in.

Let lovers wait for that last strain
of joyous music with set faces —
yet let it not be in dry places
in the sun, but after nascent rain.

PACIFIC GALE

People retreated to the beach house.
The carpenter had stopped cutting
out the port-hole on the deck side.
Sand sifted in under the door cracks.

White-maned breakers churned the beach.
Everyone was intent on doing their each.
Near dune outside drifted over tracks
wind-scattered folk had spun down.

A young man earnestly spoke of his role
in life's movie. I noticed his frown.
The hostess fumbled with the drapes.
Electricity failed. Left only shapes.

THE SUMMER OF EIGHTY FOUR

This is the Summer when brown boys grow old.
This is the season of sunshine and gold.
This is the harvest of Saticoy packing boxes,
Of fountains in courtyards and cans of cold beer.

These are the nights when boys run like foxes,
And the woes of their parents are told on a wire
That runs though the citrus groves like
Electrical messengers, enforcing desire.

Some dozens of beach games are played round a fire,
And couples steal off to make love by the dike.
This is a Summer that will never come twice,
An amorous mixture of firebrands and ice.

O! These are the days the Olympics begin!
This is the Summer to pause in one's flight.
These are the days to enjoy and delight —
Mythic, priapismic! A Summer *sans sin?*

SIERRA SPRINGTIME

These are the mountains
Called "mother,"
And last night it was as quiet
As the drowsy flowers under
The full Paschal moon.
Late night, the great valley
Moonlit, and the breasts
Of the mountains from the West
Loomed large in the light.
Not a sound but an occasional
Truck southbound on the freeway
From Fresno bearing produce
To the early morning market
In Los Angeles.

The driving is tiring and,
Rounding a hill I stop by
A side road in a glade,
Glad to have made an instant
Decision. We walk to a brook
Agleam in the moonlight.
The flowers are asleep now,
And those we have trampled
Will awake in the morning
Broken. I draw her to me
And we sink to the blossoms
On the breasts of the mountains
Called "mother."

THE FOLLOWING POEM IS FALSE!

There is a grove of gnarled oak trees on the hill
Above my home.
I focus my terrestrial telescope on them at will,
And sometimes I see them creeping down the slope,
Moving over the free-way, consuming, like smoked dope,
The houses on Vista del Mar, my street.

        Overbearing mine, slow oaks go, 'til,
A few yards longer they lurch their branches
Over sand short beach into the surf where water
Green, sunned, crabs and nudibranch, krill,
Eat and kill leathern leaves, and shocks of waves
On rocks send giant shark and dark things out
Of binding place, sea-kelp grove, treasure trove,
Across shore, uphill —

        Overbearing mine, conclaves
Of gathering porchposts and gardenswings, 'til
A few yards longer upslope, oaks sink feelers deep
And start to grow again, stronger, like live oaks
They were, and are on the hill
Above my home.

THE PRECEDING POEM IS TRUE.

THE RIGHT WORD

Where is, then, my silent voice?
Where come across clouds,
Things I see inside of me
And cannot disclose?

Must I be a fortuitous lover?
May I say, ever, "Over?"
Each inch of me lights alive.
I cannot do other.

Teach, I do —
Preach, I'd rather —
But words are merds —
Mere fertilizer.

The depth of Death
Assails my silent years,
Purloins my loins.
Still, quiet, God, I seek breath.

The candy wrappers and condoms
Are no longer there, leaching out
Their sugar and slime. Still, domes
Of thunder-clouds pile up
In the West and the cup
Of the world holds time
In its compass. We shout now
Over against dead sounds.
The Grateful Dead are
No longer grateful. The Led
Zeppelin are no longer led.

Dead is the sound of small
Dandelions trod down. Now
One tries to save the whales. All
Creatures, fond and fey, plow
Back that ancient ground.
It was not enough to rake up
Rubbers and holy smoke roaches
'Round the corners of retch.
Like Yeats, they pitched their tents
In excrement. Now our approaches
Are faltering. Now our fetch

Is far beyond our grasp.
So we leave life beyond the hasp
Of lock and look back to the brook
Of Woodstock and small waters
Trickling there where the shook
Of amplified sons and daughters
Made then upstate New York
Prime. It was a time incarnate,
When, for a while, the trod grass
In the meadow died for our sins,
And God, no doubt, *still* grins.

WELL, AFTER ALL—

Let's look at all this this way —
There are those who say
The world will be blown apart.
For those I have no heart.

Like Sirach, I incline my ear,
Not my rear, for a sign
That I may become wise
And see with clear eyes.

My sight outlongs my last —
My ear prolongs my past —
My nose seeks repose —
My tongue tastes those

For whom I feel, touch,
Stroke, poke, insert
Convert, desert, hug,
Shrug, hold, enfold.

So, with these I reveal —
May God scribe me not
Off with His awful quill.
By sense, I'm not forgot,

His will may still fulfill.

Arrowgrass blooms white and straight —
Field weeds show spare florets late —
Spring brings pained descanso —
No joy to sing of eclipses, though
Like lunaria late in Summer, moon
At Passover is worshipped with tune
Of timbrels in temples and incense
Asmoke, and blood on horns of altar.

Votive offerings of flesh, afire
With madness of thresh and intense
With heat of vernal desire
Are presented with unction. Their
Function for God is asleep in the corner,
Unknown but to those whose lunacy
Prods them. There is an uncertain

Celebration behind the temple curtain.
Ancient priest sees one unseemly seed,
Profligate, of many scattered in haste.
Out of bounty promised by Spring,
There is naught but prodigal waste.

GAFFE

There was this thing going on between the candlesticks:
The ratatouille rested there,
Red peppers gleaming among the zucchini.
The conversation was embroidered with wine,
And a deft remark caught on toothpicks
Shattered the limpid air
As though a surreptitious genie
Had erupted.

Unavoidably uttered, mine was a prime
Example of words loosely strewn
By a tongue out of tune
With the time and the temper of food.
Lightly uttered, split words were rude
And sensitive knives recoiled
From the salad, lightly oiled.

I picked up my buttered roll with a smile
And thirsted for the gift of tongues.

I need time to come down
Hard on tears shed and
Secrets told. Now, lets
Hammer it down — with nails.

Ordinary artifacts — arranged,
Glasses on counter —
The encounter —
Words exchanged.

Like some unforeseen car
On foreshore of wet mice
Encumbrances of telephone
Numbers stalk, unrecalled.

Cat reads, — licking feet.
Cookies burn in oven,
Unheeded. One more treat
Gone, burned up! A hoven.

Tears brim by trifocals.
Scarlet runner beans ripen.
She tells me to sickle.
"They're not worth a nickel

If they don't get picked."
A sickle's not like a sledge.
Sickles get nicked, but
Hammers have no edge.

Nails bite and scratch.
Bake the cookies. Climb the peak.
Nail it down. Catch the snatch.
No one knows that I am weak.

Le Grison.

SOUL

Soul is slender cord.
Wan as willow, still will
It support frame of flesh,
Unruly though senses be.

Soul seeks tender Lord.
While host wallows it will
Fill interstices, mesh sense,
And, like light's lenses, see.

Soul perceives by eye,
Sees by ear, hears by taste,
Smells by touch. In mind
Celebrates much.

Soul has own inner domain,
Spontaneous, free from logic.
Body, faulted, does remain
Beholden to soul's metaphysic.

Soul, Me, and Body — too,
Are unduly cemented,
Conjoined by God, slim. Few
Men, unruly, are not demened.

TAKE TO THE RAFT, BOYS!

The willows low below the levee wave
Lazily in the winsome wind. Jessica
Has just placed a flask of cool white wine,
(Afraid of the heat of the day) in
The cave behind, where Tom Sawyer
And Huckleberry Finn used to snatch
After Becky Thatch — "Her was a neat gurl!"
But, Boys go off for evidences of Ju-
venal sexuality and encounter, (natch!)

A very gentle man, an ancient professor
Of Classics who collected old guns,
Pornographic videos, and had, added on,
Left a shrewish wife one day it seems,
To float away on his own raft, madded ones
Not deft enough, to chase his dreams
Of youth. Left to caress only his fire-arms.
So, on slimsome raft, later boys float away,
Not wishing to be molested by heavy-
Handed words like "arrested," for that is
What it was in their raging stage
Of development. Arrested? Contested, I guess.

Still, juvenile is like the Nile — long
Flowing, and, again a ventured guess,
With small hope of egress from swamps
Of certitude and sophmoric surliness.
It was not with tumescnce and such,
Or the matter of Nietzsche, that the boys
Had arranged their toys, but the hope,
The succulent hope, that somewhere, just
Somewhere in Arcady might be some charm,
That there might be an 'Arranger,'
A man without danger, who could both
Quaff the wine that Jessica left, and sated,
Would have let them out into manhood.

The willows low below the levee wave
Lazy leaves in the winsome wind, much
More differently than the wind intended.

METATAXIS

I love the smell of asphodel.
O, asphodels do not smell?
Well, what have you to offer me
In place? A lovely blue-bell?

Another sort of wandering is
An angular joint of a boy.
That for me a metataxis,
A different sort of joy.

ANOTHER METAPHYSIC

O limpid pen!
Slit-pointed agent —
Through you I vent
My soul. A black
Extension of hand,
You are the only tool
I've got to mediate
Between reality —
And that which
None of us at all
Has . . .

Except, perhaps, in grim
Pursuit, the fool
Who flits upon a ball.

Or else — why flail
With pen of metal,
Or of felt — so quick?

My computer writes
For God
Another meaphysic.

KADDISH

Your ways, O God, are to me most incomprehensible.
This should be a surprise?
All down the long river of days and years
Your chosen people have shed bitter tears.

For what?
That a babe dies, a man, a nation?
For what does one weep? Like Job, is man's lot
Not to ask, not to question?

How dare you contend with ME?" asked Yahweh.
So, in simple submission, I reply,
Yes, dear God, if indeed you are that dear,
It is You I fear. But, let me make this clear —

Beteween the beginning and end of life
There is the life!
So one man dies, *an echte Mensch.*
Ah, noo, so look on him kindly
Dear, fearsome God.

True man tries, defines, refines Your Law.
So, God, I implore You, while I thank You
For one small slot in eternity to enjoy
Life.

True men try, comply, — defy Your Law
At their peril. Still
The beauty of Your creation is beyond compare —
Your Earth, mountains, streams, oceans.

Your flowers, fields, all sorts of things —
Show me You have given man a small carrot to nibble on.
So, one puts away empiric notions of Babylon
And succumbs.

So one more just man has died!
Please, Adonai, take his small breath of life
Into your unknown constellation,
This true man, Rosenman.

Out of the muck and mire
I took a flint rock
And another, and struck
Rock on rock —
A spark cracked forth —
Then there was fire.
My animal brain
Received a shock
From which I never
Recovered.

I crept, then ran
Across the earth
And became a man.
Whenever in
Interstices of ages
I raised my eyes,
I imprinted my hand.
In a cave in Auvergne
You heard my cries.

Now I stand
Fully erect
Before You, Maker
Of bison, grass, seas,
Great apes, ice caps, trees.
I, Man, took You, God,
Into Me.
Or — did You, over all life,
Take Me into Thee?

PATRONS

I AM PROFOUNDLY IN YOUR DEBT. You had the faith to support my first book, sight unseen. I find sufficient words of thanks hard to come by.

You represent America, from Hawaii, California and the Pacific Northwest to New York, New England, — and old England, too! You represent all walks of life. Among you are students and professors, musicians and artists, physicians and physicists, the clergy and representatives of a variety of professions. You span years from 24 to 94!

I am most grateful to all of you. This honor roll is but a small salute. Thank you all for your faith, hope and love. *Gratias agimus tibi, Domini!*

Anonymous
Pearl Anshell
Regina Austin, M. D.

Dorothy and Stanley Barr
Mrs. A. A. Birdick
Donald and Sandra Bostrom
The Maria Branzuela children
Clark C. Brown, Ph. D.
Frederick and Rebecca Burnham

Lynn and Phyllis Clifford
Reverend Charles G. Crosse
Christopher Curzon
Elliott and Ladonna Curzon
Peter Curzon

Elizabeth Ann Day
Phyllis K. De'Ath
Sauny Dills

Guerrero Espinoza

Michael Famularo, M. D.
Rita M. Fuszek

Gallerie Machbitz
Katherine S. Gittes, Ph. D.
Rosalie Gjerde

Alice Hannula
Doris and Tony Harry
Melvin and Daphne Hill
Joanna Hodges
Dorothe and Richard Horttor
Kathryn B. Hull
Virginia N. Huston

James Rodney Jee
Louise L. Jesse

Kevin Kelly
Ray, *in memoriam*, and Florence Konecke

Dimitrie and Joanne Leivici
William T. Little, Ph. D.
Carl and Wilma Locke
Nellie Hill Lolmaugh

Marian and Jerry Main
Miriam C. Maloy
Maria Martinez
Guenther and Anneliese Mayer-Harnisch, M. D.
Jim and Charlotte McGrath
Carole McHugh
Michael McLarney
Gary J. Miller

Dr. John L. Norman

Jim and Joyce Rae
Charles L. Ramsden
Craig Rees
Mona G. Rosenman, Ph. D.
Jeffrey and Diane Russell

Katy and Bob Schuh
Warren and Ellen Sevander
Reverend and Mrs. David A. Smiley
Carol Snell
Clare Spring
Richard Stanford
Russell Stepan
Juli and David Stuve

William and Susan Taber
L'rayne Teasdale
David and Virginia Tom
Mary Turnbull

Lyndon and Janice M. R. Vivrette

Vera Waegele, M. D.
Richard J. Weidner and Neemong Lee
Alice and Orville Whitcher
Lorraine Wiech

The type used in this book was composed
on the Linotype and is 11 point Jansen.
The book is printed on acid-free
paper in an edition of 400 numbered
and signed copies. The binding was done
by hand using leather on the
spine and French marble on the boards
and as end-sheets.

This is

copy

No. *(one of 400)*
not numbered
(special)

*For the good people
of St. Stephens Church
June 17, 1993*

Gordon Curzon